Unleash Your Light

Access the Divine Within You

li Cara

Unleash Your Light: Access the Divine Within You
By li Cara

Williamsburg, VA

All rights reserved.
Copyright 2019 li Cara

Illustrations by Donavin Carattini

ISBN 978-1-939696-54-0 (paperback)
ISBN 978-1-939696-57-1 (eBook)
Library of Congress Control Number: 2019952456

Printed in the U.S.A.

Scripture taken from the Amplified Bible, Copyright © 2015 by The Lockman Foundation. Used by permission.

Introduction	1
The Light Within	5
Spark of Life	10
What is the Light?	18
What is Love?	22
Seek the Light	29
You Are Not Alone	33
Be Nice to Others	37
Be Nice to Yourself	42
Combating Negative Thoughts	43
Forgiveness	47
Release your Past	48
Forgive Others	51
Forgive Yourself	60
Ignore Your Feelings	67
Set Your Mind	74
Have Faith	80
Hang in There	84
About the Author	88
See excerpt from Simple Spirituality of Self	90

Introduction

A barrage of self-help books has been written in the past 30 years. People are trying desperately to find answers to the trials and tribulations of their life. They want the antidote for the stress of day to day living, the struggle of financial burden and the baggage they carry from childhood, relationships, break ups and heartache.

I struggled with depression and self-esteem issues for most of my life. For as long as I can remember, I felt like there was something wrong with me—like everyone could see how broken I was. I felt repulsive and masculine. I just knew that everyone around me could see how wrong I was.

I wore these like a badge on my forehead:

> *UNWANTED*
> *DAMAGED*
> *BROKEN*
> *UNLOVED*

I lived my life wearing a mask.

> *Put on the mask—go to work—smile—be perky.*
>
> *Put on the mask—be a happy mom.*
>
> *Put on the mask—be a happy daughter.*
>
> *Put on the mask—be a happy wife.*

All the while, I was being eaten alive by darkness inside, constantly searching for a solution, always reading the latest self-help book, watching all the talk shows on leading a happy positive life.

I had read so much, ranging from technical psychology texts to new-age chakra crystal alignments. None of these made a difference in my life. None of them actually sunk in. One day, I literally asked the Universe for help. I offered to serve the Light.

Like a lightning bolt, my body was flooded with electricity, tingling golden light and a feeling of love like I have never felt before. I decided right then and there that I would serve the Light however I could. I wanted to feel that way every day, all the time. Over the next few days, this entire book was "downloaded" to me. I was directed to go back to the things I had read. I was led to Bible passages. I wrote and wrote and wrote.

As I connected the dots, I found many common denominators between the self-help books and religious texts, a connection and sameness centering around a few common themes. Basically, a million different methods to get across the same answers, and the more I read, the more similarities I saw. All the while, I was asking the Universe for guidance—asking to see and know the truth, asking to overcome and understand my own issues.

The fact that the information was so similar confirms to me all of the messages I've received from the Light. Every message was the same. Every message has the same point.

> *Our purpose here on Earth is to learn, to grow, to overcome our issues, to love, to be loved, to embrace unconditional love for others, to embrace unconditional love for ourselves, to connect with the Divine Light within us.*

Each religion was created with the same purpose: to guide us to the Light.

The Light Within

Words have power, especially words that have been used over and over again in worship and in prayer. The words and passages that have been used for thousands of years have the power to help you embrace empathy and unconditional love and Unleash Your Light. The words are often remembered by our souls and cells and can work like a tonic to soothe us and to lift us. Using the words that have been repeated for generations can amplify your goals and help you achieve that direct connection to the Light.

The more I applied what I was learning to myself, the more I understood how my behaviors and issues affect me. I began shifting my perspectives, changing my habits, adjusting my actions and reorganizing how I reacted to certain situations. Each step was bringing me closer to the Divine, closer to the Light, closer to my true self, closer to the path the Universe wants me to walk and my true purpose here on Earth.

As I continued to strip away the layers of darkness and negativity, I began to feel the Light working in my life. The more I dug into my own patterns, the more things started to line up in front of me. The more darkness and pain I lost, the more joy and love I gained.

The more love and joy I gained, the easier it was to make that connection to the Light, to God, to the Divine, to the Source, to the Universe. It doesn't matter what you call it, as long as you are seeking.

Unleash Your Light is all about breaking through and overcoming the emotional obstacles that keep us separated from the Divine that dwells within each one of us. By applying the simple—but not easy—steps of Unleash Your Light, I have accomplished a direct connection to the Divine Light, and it has changed me to the core.

Some of us have tried to find this connection through religion. However, not everyone feels a connection to religion. Some of us have been so disillusioned by what organized religion has become. Others have been excluded by the church. Some have never believed.

Guess what? It doesn't matter! The Light doesn't actually need religion to transform you.

The Light is already inside of each of us from birth. By learning how to access and Unleash Your Light, you can make a direct connection to the Divine, the source of all creation, the Light of the Universe. It will change your life and transform you. You will be able to live your true purpose here on Earth and create the life your soul was created for.

Let's get straight to the point.

> *Do you believe in a higher power?*
>
> *Do you believe that there is some benevolent or perhaps uncaring force out there watching over us?*
>
> *Would you say you believe in God, the Bible, Jesus Christ, the Holy Spirit, the whole nine yards?*
>
> *Do you believe in God but don't really feel right identifying with any particular religion?*
>
> *Are you are disgusted by the church scandals and have given up religion?*
>
> *Do you go to church every week, but never seem to get the comfort from it that you see others receive?*

Are you questioning whether deep down you really don't believe in God?

Do you feel the world is entirely random?

Whichever one of these situations fits you, it doesn't matter. You can be, or not be, any religion you want and still seek the Light. If you are looking for that comfort, that forgiveness, that calm, peaceful, joyful life; then you are looking for the Light. You are seeking peace and clarity, love and joy.

You, my friend, are seeking the Light!

Take time to answer these questions:

What am I?

What is a soul?

What is God?

How does it feel to embrace your Divine?

Spark of Life

What am I?

Interesting question, eh? Ask yourself. *What am I?*

> *Did you describe yourself in appearance? (I'm a cute redhead.)*
>
> *Did you identify with your name or occupation? (I am a lawyer.)*
>
> *Perhaps you said, "I am a mother."*

We'll come back to this identification in just a moment.

Let me pose another perspective...

> *I am an immortal piece of the Creator, living in a mortal, physical body.*
>
> *I am a microcosm of the macrocosm.*

I am a singular expression of a plurality.

What the heck does that mean? To answer, I pose yet another question: do you believe in a soul?

Some people and religions believe the soul carries the essence of a person, and without a soul you die. Stories of the souls of sinners being black with their deeds have been told for eons, before the records of our history. Stories of reincarnation; people, like me, who remember past lives; and child prodigies who can play piano with the masters at five years old.

These things support the existence of a soul that dwells within each of us. A soul that cannot be destroyed and is incarnated in a mortal vessel repeatedly.

How does the mortal body work? We know when the heart stops pumping and the brain stops working, the body dies. We are mortal. Our bodies are made of flesh and blood which deteriorates over time.

But, this body—this human body—is a masterpiece of intricacy, with all parts of the body completing its own functions controlled by the brain. Much of this is involuntary: breathing, processing food, circulating blood, etc.

Some of what the brain does is voluntary: I'm going to go to work now, I'm making something to eat, I'm walking over here, etc. The brain function *we* are most aware of is the thinking part. That constant narration that dictates how you feel and how you act; it tries to define who you are internally.

So, *how* does the brain do this processing? How does it make the body complete these functions? How does it send these messages to the moving parts?

The brain uses electricity. It sends electrical currents through our nervous system, which tell the bits and pieces what to do. Modern equipment used to monitor brain activity displays the level of electricity in the brain. That electricity is *literally* the spark of life.

Take time to answer this question:

How do I define myself?

Is that my soul?

Many believe that that spark of electricity in our brain is the soul, and after each death, the soul chooses to reincarnate and live another lifetime. Others believe that when we die, we rot in the ground. The End. Actually, both are right, but I will take it a step further.

Energy cannot be destroyed; it can only change form. So, when that little bit of electricity in our brains, the spark that gives us life, is no longer with us, it must still exist in some form. I believe that it returns to the whole—to the Creator Energy.

The soul, the energy, the spark of life transforms itself into the great beyond.

The great beyond, which is unknown to us when we are mortal in our vessel, is the knowledge stored deep in the memory banks of our soul. I believe this is not only proof of existence beyond death, but the proof that we are eternal; that our energy goes on and on. We are all a part of a larger whole.

Am I Really Connected to You?

The simple answer? Yes, but let's go backward a little bit to go forward.

I have established that the mortal body is inhabited and animated by a bit of electricity that some people call a soul, or at the very least, is an undefinable, indestructible entity of some sort. The electricity that animates us comes from the same source. That source is the Creator, who literally sends a piece of its own life force, to inhabit the tiny human mortals we grow in our womb. When we die, the piece of the Creator that animated us, returns to itself.

So, the spark of life that animates you comes from the same Creator/Source that gave me a spark of its animating life source. In this way, yes, we are all connected. The Bible actually supports this by saying we are all God's children. If the Holy Spirit dwells within us, then we must be connected to each other, right?

1 Corinthians 3:16 states, "Do you not know that you are a temple of God and the Spirit of God dwells in you?"

Each of us is a temple of God and the Spirit of God is within each of us. That 'Spirit of God' is the direct connection to Light/Source/God. Accessing that connection is how you shift your life into the Light. Embracing that belief is the true purpose of our life. It is the beginning of the transformation.

To accept that we are *not* damaged sinners and accept we are the caretakers of Divine Light. We are the carriers of the Spirit of God. Acknowledging this responsibility, embracing this mission and shifting your perception of your own personal path through this life will unlock your connection to Divine and Unleash Your Light.

Take time to answer this question:

What do you hope to gain from seeking the light?

What is the Light?

The Light is the Creator. The Light is that spark of energy that animates and connects each of us. The Light is the love the Creator feels for us because we are brought to life by the Creator's very essence. The Light animates each and every one of us. If you can make that connection directly to the Divine that dwells within our life force, you can find joy and peace in your life.

The Light is God. The Light of the Universe is the higher power that has given us life. We can all access and harness that Light, because a piece of it lives inside of us. You can make the connection directly to God by accessing that Light. You can cut out the messy middlemen of religions and traditions. You can directly access the wisdom, strength, power and love of our Creator, just by accessing and unleashing your Light.

How will this affect me?

Well, the honest answer is that since I don't know you personally, I can't specifically tell you how this knowledge will affect your life.

You may start being a little nicer to that grumpy convenience store clerk. Maybe you will start to feel a little better, a little less alone. I do know that if you actually take each step on the road as it comes, it will be transformative. It can shift your thoughts, change your life, and attract more positivity into your life. The more in touch you are with the Light, the more your path will be revealed, the more your destiny will be laid out in front of you.

How do I want it to affect you?

I want you to Unleash Your Light.

I want you to try to find peace in your life.

I want people who aren't religious to be able to regain their faith in a higher power and a purpose to life.

I want you to seek God.

I want you to establish your own direct line to the wisdom of the Creator/Light/Source.

Let me tell you, when your mind isn't bogged down with the junk and darkness we carry with us, the messages and guidance of the Light is really clear. It can't be mistaken for anything but the Light working in your life.

There is a higher power.

Even many of those who are not religious can agree there is something bigger than us, a presence that is sometimes palpable in those quiet moments of peace that are so few and far between.

When you seek out that Light, that power, something changes inside of you. Something essential that changes you to your core. The Light is literally transforming. This is often referred to in many religious texts.

God has 9,000 names. Use whatever feels right for you. Many connect best through the structure of Christianity. Others are immediately put off by the word God. Spirituality in general is about the message, not the messenger, so whatever feels right to you, is right—God/Source/Creator/Sophia Gaia/Light. Call it Fred. It doesn't matter what name you call "God," as long as you are seeking.

When you seek the Light, it isn't a physical trip. It's not somewhere you go or something you see. It's a shift inside of you. Seeking the Light is something you will do for the rest of your life, until your death when you will be reunited with the Light.

What's the purpose of seeking the Light?

Life. Life is the purpose, and the purpose of this life is to seek the Light—to experience love and peace, to work through personal issues, to experience pain and hurt and allow it to elevate us and not drag us down. When you seek the Light, your true purpose will be revealed. When you seek the Light, you will feel real joy and true peace.

So, how do I seek the Light?

There are many paths to the Light, but they are all paved with love. That sounds cheesy, right? Cheesy, but true. The way to find the Light is to always walk in love. Does this mean walk around like a hippie dippy Pollyanna constantly spouting annoyingly cheerful quotes? Maybe for some people, but not for most.

Walking in love means you always forgive.

You always speak in a kind, loving way.

You think in a kind, loving way.

You act from love and make decisions from a place of love.

What is Love?

Before we can talk about what love is, we should talk about what it isn't. All actions and emotions come from two things: love and fear. How can you tell the difference? Anything that does not come from a place of love is based in fear and is not the right action on the path towards the Light.

Going a little deeper, fear is created through losing love or lack of love. The fear of losing love/approval is a powerful motivator, often creating visceral anger and lashing out behavior.

Unconditional love is the frequency of the Universe. The emotion of unconditional love literally creates a brain wave that is at the same frequency as deep space. Utilizing that frequency allows you to fully embrace your own Divine nature. Embracing that Divine connection with others allows us to experience that love in a profound way.

The love you receive from others comes directly from the Light, directly from the Creator Energy. It comes directly from God.

Everyone has felt that emotion at least once in their life. The feeling of complete bliss, maybe looking into your baby's eyes, watching your child sleep, or gazing into the eyes of your true love. The feeling when you look at a puppy. That loving, gentle, peaceful, emotional, tear-inducing, overwhelming feeling.

In that moment, that is a direct connection to the Light, the Source, the Creator, God, or whatever you may call it. That feeling is a direct connection to that higher power, higher vibration, existing in all encompassing, all forgiving love, that moment of bliss where you are totally in the now.

You should strive for that connection every moment in your life. Live in love and walk in Light; those are the moments in which you are closest to God.

Every action you take should contain that love, that emotion. You should live your life every moment trying to walk in that emotion each day of your life. Look at every person as if they are precious to you, as they should be. We are all anointed by pieces of the whole. The energy, the spark that animates our minds and bodies, is our Creator manifested inside of each and every living thing.

To go through life in a state of happiness and peace will change the world we live in. We could create Nirvana on earth just by shifting the global consciousness to one of mercy and compassion. People living in peace with enough for everyone. No poverty, no fighting, no wars. It is possible; it is real. We have to overpower the thinking that blocks this goal.

Some call it the darkness. Psychology calls it the ego. Christianity calls it being tempted by the devil or the spirit of the anti-Christ.

The darkness we all carry is made up of junk we have accepted as truth about ourselves. We process it as self-hatred, clinging to it to the point of self-sabotage.

Our spiritual purpose is to overcome the darkness, the trauma, the suffering. We must learn to accept and then shine Light on that darkness. Expose your darkness to the Light of Unconditional Love, Forgiveness and Empathy, sending love and forgiveness to the ones who contributed to your darkness.

We live in a constant duality between our human emotions and our Divine Light. Balancing this duality, accepting the Human *and* the Divine, and embracing living with both is exactly our journey.

This can be easier said than done.

You must learn to be vigilant because, as anyone who carries it in grief and depression can tell you, the darkness is comforting.

It's comfortable; the darkness soothes you. It tells you what you want to hear, justifying your wrongs, keeping you the victim of all situations. It will beckon you to escape the pain of living, which is created by this darkness, feeds you lies about yourself and your self-worth (yes, Yoda was right).

The darkness spent a lifetime whispering garbage and lies, telling you that you will fail. *Don't bother trying... Don't hope... You will fail anyway... Don't fall in love, you'll just mess it up...*

Those are the things the darkness has cultivated. Those thoughts that plague you and keep you separated from love and life, keep you separated from the direct connection with the Creator.

That darkness has been working your whole life to take you down. The darker and more depressed you become, the tighter the hold the darkness has on you. When you live in that narcissistic darkness, you miss the point of our existence here on Earth, which is to ascend, as a species, to a higher vibration of life. Staying in the darkness is a choice.

Now...shift your perception for a moment.

Where does this *darkness* come from?

If it's created by my own pain and suffering, then aren't I the darkness? Haven't I created this darkness?

How did I create the darkness?

Our darkness, our wounds, our destructive patterns are created through our lives in response to painful and stressful situations. It became a self-defense mechanism to protect ourselves from harm. If you have a temper and curse out those you love, it's probably a habit you created to protect yourself from losing those you love. The solution? Push people away so you don't get close enough to be sad when they go away.

We have to accept our self-defense mechanisms, even as we disassemble them. Thank them for protecting us all these years but let them know we no longer need them. We are choosing differently now.

You may say, "Choice? I'm not choosing to be sad or miserable. Are you crazy? Who would choose this?"

It may not be a conscious choice to fall into the darkness, but if you choose not to make a change, if you choose not to try, if you purposefully turn away from the light at the end of the tunnel, *that* is where the choice comes in. That is where your ego comes in.

Your ego will try to keep you in darkness, just to prove its theories right. The ego will set you up to fail over and over again so it can say, "See? I was right. You are a loser. Your life is garbage."

Your darkness is customized just for you—it knows your weaknesses, and it pushes all of your buttons. Your darkness will do just about anything to win. The battle within each of us is the ultimate battle between good and evil, which is our sole purpose here on Earth. It is an integration of the energy of unconditional love into our human experience. We are to overcome our issues here on Earth, in life after life, until more of us become enlightened, awakened, aware, connected and loving, so we can exist in that ever-loving state of life and peace: Nirvana.

Our lives here are beautiful, amazing, and incredible. We have a beautiful planet filled with astonishing and wondrous experiences in the physical realm. Our planet is the Garden of Eden.

Even in our trials, we are blessed with the opportunity to walk through this life and learn from it. We can explore and enlighten ourselves. Even in our darkness, we have the chance to embrace the Light. In fact, the point of the darkness is to learn to embrace the Light.

It's never too late to turn towards the Light and to make a direct connection with God. No matter how dark your sins, God/Source/Creator/Light welcomes you with open arms. The Light embraces you with warmth and love. You can change your entire life in an instant. Reject the darkness and invite the Light into your heart.

Seek the Light

How do we drive out of the deep dark pit of depression and walk in the Light again?

Seek the Light.

You must seek the Light in every moment of your life.

When you seek the Light, you try to always act and think from love.

Don't act in anger.

Don't think mean or hurtful things about yourself or others.

How do we do that correctly?

These thoughts come organically, right? Nobody wants to be angry enough to hit anybody. Nobody wants to feel depressed, right? Yet, we allow the littlest things to control our emotions like slow drivers, rude people, disrespectful kids, etc.

Every time you have a thought like that, stop yourself, put a positive spin on it, and reject it.

"No, I don't believe everyone is out to get me."

"No, I am not destined to fail. I'm just running into obstacles that are preparing me for big future success."

This may sound a little crazy. It may sound counterintuitive, but you must say it; you must correct the thought or deed. Implant the loving thought and reject the non-loving thought. Replace that with a loving thought, "I'm not stupid. I just forgot." And forgive yourself.

Talk to yourself like you are your own best friend. Be comforting and supportive and reject the negative judgements as untrue. Right action begins with right thoughts. When you are thinking right, your life begins to flow in a way that brings you to your true purpose and happiness. The more you maintain a positive, loving mind, the more the way to fulfillment will open to you.

The perfect job, the right partner, the chance to follow your dream.

It all comes from everything lining up just right. The closer you can live to the Light, the more doors open to us, showing us the way we can live our life's calling—our true purpose.

When we focus more on enlightenment, we can cultivate that direct connection with the Light, the Creator, the Source, God or whatever you may call it.

When you seek the Light, the Light is seeking you.

When the Light finds you and you recognize it, it will change your heart, your life and your world.

When you Unleash Your Light, you will transform yourself and the world around you.

Take time to answer these questions:

How does the darkness show itself in your life?

What feelings does that darkness cultivate?

Why do you think it affects you in this way?

You Are Not Alone

If we can all access the Creator directly, then we can work together, united by His life force, to recreate the paradise of the Garden of Eden here on Earth.

How do we do this? How do we figure out how to connect directly to the Creator? Maybe you feel there is no way for you to do this. Maybe you feel a life of peace, love and joy will never be yours. Do you feel life is hopeless, or that you are all alone in this world?

You are not alone.

We all feel alone sometimes. Some of us feel alone all the time. Some of us feel alone in a roomful of people. I understand that feeling because I felt the same way. The almost crippling feeling that nobody really loves us, really knows us, really *sees* us...

There is a knowing that comes with accepting that a piece of Light/Source/God is within us. It is a knowing connected deep in our heart. You must know in your heart you are never alone. God is always with you. The Light is always within you. Realizing this is the first step to Unleashing Your Light.

As a previous nonbeliever, I understand how abstract that concept can be. I look around. I see no one supporting me. I feel no one loving me. And I'm supposed to believe that Light/Source/God—some nameless, faceless entity—is with me. I could never get past the loneliness. I felt like nobody cared, understood or loved me.

Please know that Light/Source/God gets it.

God really does understand. God really does care. God really does love you. God is within you. You are an expression of God. Embrace the Divine in you and Unleash Your Light.

How do I know?

I know because I went through a transformation.

My whole life has changed. My heart has changed. My mind has changed.

I am not alone.

I am the beloved of the Light (and so are you!).

Now, I always feel the presence of the Light.

How did I get here?

How did I go from being a non-believing, depressed and miserable to here...a peaceful, joyful, happy, beloved believer? It was actually so simple, it made me want to kick myself because I went 41 years without it.

I prayed. I asked Light/Source/God for forgiveness. The answer I got was this book, these steps, this flood of knowledge and wisdom beyond my own experiences. I promised Light/Source/God that from this day out, I would do my best to live through unconditional love. I promised God I would serve the Light however I am able. I asked Light/Source/God to change my heart. I asked Light/Source/God to help me to feel loved.

Immediately, this tingly feeling of peace and love came over me. And since that day, I can bring that feeling back at a moment's notice to recharge me.

Now, when I feel sad and alone, I take a minute to close my eyes, take a deep breath and just feel the love of Light/Source/God pouring down over my head like a shower of light and energy.

I am never alone, and neither are you.

Anytime you need reassurance, just ask. Ask the Light to help you feel loved. Ask Source to help you feel its presence. Read over these Scriptures to help you stay focused and feel the presence of Light/Source/God in your life.

Psalm 136:1: "Give thanks to the Lord, for He is good. His love endures forever."

Psalm 146:8: "The Lord gives sight to the blind, the Lord lifts up those who are bowed down, the Lord loves the righteous."

II Samuel 22:29-31: "You, Lord, are my Lamp; the Lord turns my darkness into light."

Be Nice to Others

Be nice to others.

I know what you're thinking.

Be nice? That's your advice?

Yes! That's my advice. It seems like simple common sense. Be nice. But often, we are not nice to one another.

Maybe the cashier at the grocery store made a mistake. You got annoyed and rude. Perhaps you even made a rude comment like, "How hard is it to push buttons?"

When someone cuts you off in traffic, does a string of curse words flow from your lips or do you flip them off? Maybe you start chasing them through traffic. Road rage, anyone?

It's not always easy. It's a choice. There's a moment when you are about to react.

Choose to be a blessing.

Choose to be nice.

You might make a difference in the other person's life. Maybe they are having trials in their life and your smile and understanding can give them a moment of peace or brighten their day.

Give them hope. It can be difficult at times, but the blessings you give will come back to you.

Every single person you encounter is connected to you. They hold a piece of the Divine Light within them, just like you do!

They are a reflection of you and your issues. Sometimes it's your reaction you need to examine. Sometimes they are literally mirroring your own baggage back to you.

The old saying, "We always dislike in others what we dislike in ourselves" is often very true.

I have found that these interactions are a gift. They allow me to view those places in me that need some love and healing. Anything that provokes a strong reaction in me is a clue to an unhealed wound. By paying attention to these places, I'm able to really dig into the issue and process it properly with love and forgiveness.

Matthew 5:44-48: "But I tell you, love your enemies and pray for those who persecute you, that you may be children of your Father in heaven. He causes his sun to rise on the evil and the good and sends rain on the righteous and the unrighteous. If you love those who love you, what reward will you get? Are not even the tax collectors doing that? And if you greet only your own people, what are you doing more than others? Do not even pagans do that? Be perfect, therefore, as your heavenly Father is perfect.

1 John 4:20: "Whoever claims to love God yet hates a brother or sister is a liar. For whoever does not love their brother and sister, whom they have seen, cannot love God, whom they have not seen."

Philippians 2:5: "In your relationships with one another, have the same mindset as Christ Jesus."

Ephesians 2:10: "For we are God's handiwork, created in Christ Jesus to do good works, which God prepared in advance for us to do."

2 Corinthians 9:7: "Each of you should give what you have decided in your heart to give, not reluctantly or under compulsion, for God loves a cheerful giver."

Colossians 3:12: "Therefore, as God's chosen people, holy and dearly loved, clothe yourselves with compassion, kindness, humility, gentleness and patience."

Take time to answer these questions:

What can you do to start this practice?

Do you think this will affect your life?

Be Nice to Yourself

The other half of the equation is not so easy.

Be nice to yourself.

Sounds simple... deceptively simple, but it's harder than you think.

When you look in the mirror, what do you say to yourself? Do you smile and think how great you look, or do you zero in on "faults" you see staring back at you? Do a chorus of voices ring out in your head calling you ugly, fat and stupid?

When you make a mistake, do you condemn yourself a failure, loser, or no good?

You would never say that to your best friend.

You would never put up with someone else saying that to your best friend.

Before you judge yourself, call yourself names or are mean and hateful to yourself, take a minute and say something nice. I know it's hard.

Maybe you don't really believe what you are saying, but if you say it enough, it will become your truth. Why? The Divine Light within us already embraces and knows how amazing we are. It's the part of us that is created by our trauma, our suffering, and the lives we have led that judges us, insults us and holds onto these negative beliefs about ourselves.

It won't always be easy. If you catch yourself being mean, then correct yourself and say something nice. It will become a habit.

I know this from personal experience. I couldn't even pass a mirror without saying I was a fat, ugly loser. No one would ever really love me.

But I overcame it day by day, week by week… and you can too.

Combating Negative Thoughts

We are born pure and perfect. We are the closest to the Light at the moment of our birth. As we live, each day of our life begins to taint us, adding layers of abuse, pain and hurt. Eventually we end up with a running inner dialogue, voices criticizing and scolding us for everything we do.

Television personality Dr. Phil calls them ANTS: Automatic Negative Thoughts. Traditional psychology calls those voices the negative ego. Some would call the voices demons or the devil.

Author and Spiritual Leader Eckhart Tolle speaks of the moment in an argument where, even though we may still be yelling at the person across from us, we are able to observe ourselves too.

The fact that we can lean back and listen to those voices means they are a separate energy from ourselves, from our Divine center. They are created by the pain, trauma and suffering you have experienced.

Those voices are not your Divine self. They are something else entirely. The voices can be loud and convincing, trying to hold you down and keep you from your true potential. They will sabotage you and keep you from experiencing unconditional love in its purest form. Those voices will torture you; trying to get you feel fear, anger, hatred, toward yourself and towards others.

You must reject those voices.

When you hear them start, reject what they are saying and replace it by saying, "I am a child of the Light and I am made perfect, exactly who I need to be to accomplish my purpose in this life."

If you are about to be mean to someone because the voices start spinning about how it's not fair, they can't treat you like that, and the anger starts to build, say, "I reject that feeling. I am a child of the Light and I am a blessing to all who cross my path."

It sounds a little crazy, but it could be your purpose in that person's life to teach them forgiveness or patience. You *can* choose to be nice to yourself and others. It's tough at first, but it's like a muscle; the more you use it the stronger it gets.

Here are some inspirational scriptures and quotes to support you when you are feeling weak:

Proverb 23: "As we think, so shall we become."

"What we think, we become." – Buddha

"We are what we think. All that we are arises with our thoughts. With our thoughts, we make the world." – Buddha

"You can search throughout the entire universe for someone who is more deserving of your love and affection than you are yourself, and that person is not to be found anywhere. You yourself, as much as anybody in the entire universe deserve your love and affection." – Buddha

Take time to answer these questions

What are the negative beliefs you hold about yourself?

What are a few ways you can counter these beliefs with loving energy toward yourself?

Forgiveness

Release Your Past

Forgive Others

Forgive Yourself

These are the next three steps to Unleash Your Light. I have grouped them together because they are all intertwined. We must forgive others and ourselves fully in order to release the past. It can be incredibly difficult to let go of judgement. Society has conditioned us to categorize things as good or bad, right or wrong. And yet, we logically know that life is more complicated than that. There are so many shades of gray, as well as a rainbow of experiences out there. We are not created to carry the burden of guilt and shame. This is why so many of the world's religions have a mechanism for forgiveness. Forgiveness is one of the most difficult steps but is a vital part of the process of Awakening and the journey into Self.

Release your Past

We all have pain in our past. Someone or many someones have done us wrong. The wrong may be physical abuse from your parents or a loved one. The pain you suffered may be from verbal abuse—someone called you names, made you feel like garbage. Words scar. Words leave little memory blocks and can program you to behave a certain way, and you won't even realize it.

For example, imagine if you wrote a poem in the third grade and the teacher told you your poem was horrible and that you shouldn't make writing your day job. Something as simple as that can set up a block. From that point on, writing anything can be difficult. You expect to fail because someone years ago told you that you couldn't write.

Our minds are really like steel traps. Every negative thing said to you changes who you are. Your mind saves the negative and refers back to it over and over again.

If you were called ugly by mean kids, you look in the mirror and think you're ugly.

If parents hit you for making a mistake, you may respond by hitting others.

It's like the bad stuff clings to the inside of our brain and inside our hearts. The way to let go of these scars, these wounds from our past, is through forgiveness. The way we release our past is through forgiveness.

Easier said than done, right?

> Matthew 11:28-30: "Come to me, all you who are weary and burdened, and I will give you rest. Take my yoke upon you and learn from me, for I am gentle and humble in heart, and you will find rest for your souls. For my yoke is easy and my burden is light."

Take time to answer these questions:

What are you holding onto from your past?

Did you resolve the situation?

What are you getting from holding onto it?

Forgive Others

Sometimes we need to forgive someone who doesn't deserve it.

We all have people in our lives who have hurt us, who have crossed us, who have betrayed us. We have felt stabbed in the back, taken advantage of and downright heartbroken by people in our past who have done us wrong in a big way, or in a lot of little ways over and over again.

It hurts, and it doesn't just hurt in the moment—it can hurt for years to come. It can be something that affects your decisions every day.

When you are betrayed and get hurt, it's something that will stick with you. It stains your heart and shifts something in your brain. It can shift your perspective 180 degrees, changing who you are and how you present yourself to the world. The pain doesn't go away easily, and even when it does, there is a lesson imprinted on your psyche that you carry with you. That imprint of pain and the lesson you took away from it stays with you and affects everything you do—every decision you make, which chances you take, who you get involved with, how you react to pain, who you love, how you love, and even *if* you love.

Sometimes you don't even realize what you are doing or why you are reacting the way you do. You mess up good relationships, avoid certain types of people, stay away from situations, and push away the people who love you.

Why? Why do we hold onto the pain? Most of the time, when the initial pain passes, we think it's gone—out of sight, out of mind. We move on with our lives and leave the pain behind—or so we think. We don't want to carry this stuff around, right?

Our minds are like computers. Everything we do, everything we hear, everything we see is programmed onto our hard drive. And just like on a computer, even when you delete an app from your screen, there are still pieces of that app deep within the computer. When the betrayal or hurt happened, it installed little triggers in you.

Here's an example. You have a long-term partner/boyfriend/girlfriend. You come home from work one day, and the bed is stripped, sheets in the washer, no sign of your partner. Later you find out that your partner had another lover over at your house, in *your* bed. Of course, you break up and you move on.

So here we are two years later. You've moved on and you are in a happy loving relationship. You come home from work and you find the bed stripped, sheets in the washer, your partner folding laundry on the couch. They turn to you and smile, proud of their good deed. You fly off the handle, screaming, yelling, losing your mind. A fight ensues, and even though your partner is able to prove that they didn't have anyone at the house, now you watch their every move with suspicion. The trust in the relationship is broken and your partner leaves you. Your partner didn't even do anything wrong. There was no cheating, and yet you lost someone you loved all because of the triggers installed by your betrayal two years ago.

Those triggers will continue to plague you for the rest of your life *unless* you can figure out a way to uninstall them. How do you do that? Forgive the person who put them there.

I'm sure that you've heard the saying about how holding a grudge is like drinking poison and waiting for the other person to die. That is exactly how forgiveness works. You have to forgive the person you are holding a grudge against; it's like the antidote to the poison.

So, how do you drink the antidote? The first thing to do is figure out where your grudge lies and who hurt you. This part is going to suck—no ifs ands or buts about it. Think back to the moment you were hurt by someone.

What did they say that hurt you? What was the situation?

Now be unbiased and fair to both sides. How did you contribute to the situation? Could you have done something to prevent it?

Don't get defensive—be honest with yourself.

There is a belief that the people in our lives are a reflection of what is within each of us. The Light/God/Source is always bringing us opportunities to heal and to learn about ourselves. Each time we forgive someone, it's an opportunity to look within and examine our own behavior and our own core beliefs, both correct and incorrect. The change always starts within each of us.

Now, I want you to put yourself in the other person's shoes.

We often expect others to react the way we would react but remember the person who hurt you has lived a different life than you have. Different triggers were installed by the life they led and the experiences they have had. Maybe they hurt you because of a trigger you pulled without even realizing it. People are rarely hurtful to other people because they want to be—it's usually because of something inside of them. So when something bad happens, take your own emotion out of it. Be the observer. Try to figure it out.

The next step in the process is to be compassionate about their motivation. Have empathy for their pain and the experiences they have had in their lives. Be understanding of the triggers and possible life events that led them to treat you that way. Remember the love or friendship you had for them back when you were still on good terms. Use that feeling of empathy and connection to find your way to forgiveness for them in their time of need.

They may not even know why they hurt you, betrayed you, or lashed out at you.

Most people don't examine why they have their feelings, they just feel them. But you are going to be different. You are going to logically and compassionately talk yourself through the situation from both sides and comfort the person that hurt you, because obviously if they hurt you, they must be hurting too. You don't have to tell them in person; you don't have to call them; you don't even have to send them a message. You just forgive them and wish them well; no one has to hear it but you.

Our visualization is powerful. Some people believe we manifest reality with our thoughts and our intention. Set your mind is one of the steps of Unleash Your Light .

Set your intention on forgiving. Say it out loud. Tell that person as if they were standing in front of you that you forgive them and hope they work out their issues and find happiness. Tell them the pain they caused you has no power over you anymore and you have no use for it. Wish them well and mentally send them on their way.

Don't think you have to let that person back into your life—you don't. Forgiving is not condoning. It doesn't mean what was done is okay or right or even understandable. It just means you aren't giving it power over your life anymore, whether it's your deed or someone else's.

Forgiving is not weakness. When you forgive someone, you're really doing it for yourself, not them.

It's like running a defrag program on your computer and sweeping out all the leftover pieces of the triggers that were installed. It may take more than one attempt.

Reprogramming can take time. When you react to a trigger or think of a person who hurt you with anger or pain in your heart, just say, "I forgive you" and let it go. Forgiveness is the best thing you can do for yourself!

Proverbs 10:1: "Hatred stirs up conflict, but love covers over all wrongs."

Colossians 3:12-14: "Therefore, as God's chosen people, holy and dearly loved, clothe yourselves with compassion, kindness, humility, gentleness and patience. Bear with each other and forgive one another if any of you has a grievance against someone. Forgive as the Lord forgave you. And over all these virtues put on love, which binds them all together in perfect unity."

2 Corinthians 2:10: "Anyone you forgive, I also forgive. And what I have forgiven—if there was anything to forgive—I have forgiven in the sight of Christ for your sake."

Matthew 18:21-22: "Then Peter came to Jesus and asked, 'Lord, how many times shall I forgive my brother or sister who sins against me? Up to seven times?' Jesus answered, 'I tell you, not seven times, but seventy-seven times.'"

"Holding on to anger is like grasping a hot coal with the intent of throwing it at someone else; you are the one who gets burned." – Buddha

"We cannot embrace God's forgiveness if we are so busy clinging to past wounds and nursing old grudges." – T. D. Jakes

Take time to answer these questions:

Who do you need to forgive?

What is stopping you from forgiving them?

Forgive Yourself

Guilt eats you alive and will make you do crazy things—overcompensate, overreact. It can make you angry, depressed, violent, or over-indulgent. How can you fix this? How can you get relief from this? Conventional society says therapy. You go to therapy to talk about what happened, and the therapist tries to help you let it go.

Sound familiar? When you go to confession, you tell a priest what you did wrong, he gives you prayers to recite as an act of contrition, then you are forgiven.

What?

I just said the magic word... forgiven.

If you are forgiven, you can move forward. If you forgive the person who hurt you, then you can move on. Forgiving doesn't mean what happened was okay, but when you forgive, it gives you a chance to lift the burden off your shoulders.

Okay, let me get personal here for a minute. Some things happened to me in my early twenties that I carried around with me for years. I made a poor choice regarding custody of my three-year-old son and everything spiraled out of control. He and I have spent years repairing/living in the damage done to him while he was out of my care. He still carries the emotional scars of what happened to him.

I suffered with guilt for many years. I parented out of guilt, often excusing bad behavior, because in my mind, I was the cause of him behaving badly. In my mind, it was my fault he was taken and my fault someone else hurt him so badly.

I carried so much guilt, not only for what I did with the custody decision, but guilt over what I didn't do and the decision I should have made. I wasn't there to protect him from harm, both mental and physical. I blamed myself for the attention I didn't give my daughter because my son needed so much attention.

I carried so much pain.

How did I overcome this guilt? How did I stop beating myself up over the past?

I repented. That's the first step. I honestly admitted my part in what happened. I told Light/Source/God *and* myself I was sorry for what I did, and I asked for forgiveness. Then, I asked the Light to help me forgive myself and put the past in the past. I asked the Source to heal my pain and take the anger from me so I can focus on tomorrow and focus on serving the Light and being a blessing to others in this life.

I beat myself up over my mistakes for so many years when I didn't have to. Our minds and bodies are not designed to function properly when we carry the guilt of a lifetime of mistakes and sins along with us. That's what "Jesus died for our sins" is all about.

That portion of the Bible is designed to help us forgive ourselves and to help us unburden in a way that seems physical to us—in a way we can picture in our minds. We can unburden because Christianity tells us Jesus literally takes that weight from us. By making it a physical process we can visualize, it helps us to release our burdens. When we mess up, we are already forgiven. Jesus has taken the punishment for us.

You don't have to use the Jesus-based method if you don't feel comfortable, but you do have to learn to lift your "'sins" off your back and forgive yourself. If you aren't religious, you can try writing your sins and wrong doings down on paper. Then burn the paper as you say out loud. "I forgive myself. I forgive the person who hurt me."

You can do this as many times as you need to. Each time you should feel lighter, brighter and closer to full and true forgiveness. This helps in forgiving others as well. Write down what was done to you and burn it as you forgive that person.

Forgiving yourself is loving yourself. Again, sounds simple but can be difficult in practice. You are a Divine child of the Light. Even when you mess up, make mistakes, and make bad choices, you are forgiven as soon as you are sorry. You have to love yourself more than you feel the need to punish yourself.

Don't punish yourself anymore.

Is it easy to let it go? No. Is it a struggle every day? Yes.

Anytime you feel yourself slipping, punishing, or self-hating, you have to take a moment.

Self-correct and be nice to yourself (remember that step?).

Talk to yourself. You are your own best friend. You made a mistake, but you learned from it—you repented. Don't keep reliving the pain. Don't keep beating yourself up. You are a good person with a good heart.

Know that if you are truly sorry, then you are truly forgiven. Know that if you forgive those who hurt you, then that memory can no longer hurt you.

When you don't forgive, you let that person or that incident torture you for the rest of your life. It's not easy but it's doable. If you set your mind and have faith, you can do it.

Need help? Ask the Light. Ask for support; reach out to others for support. Help someone else, be a blessing. Forgiveness doesn't come easy, but it is one of the best things you can do for yourself.

1 John 1:9: "If we confess our sins, he is faithful and just and will forgive us our sins and purify us from all unrighteousness."

Ephesians 1:7: "In him we have redemption through his blood, the forgiveness of sins, in accordance with the riches of God's grace."

Romans 5:3-4: "Not only so, but we also glory in our sufferings, because we know that suffering produces perseverance; perseverance, character; and character, hope."

"The weak can never forgive. Forgiveness is the attribute of the strong." – Mahatma Gandhi

"We must develop and maintain the capacity to forgive. He who is devoid of the power to forgive is devoid of the power to love. There is some good in the worst of us and some evil in the best of us. When we discover this, we are less prone to hate our enemies." – Martin Luther King, Jr.

"The practice of forgiveness is our most important contribution to the healing of the world." – Marianne Williamson

"We think that forgiveness is weakness, but it's absolutely not; it takes a very strong person to forgive." – T. D. Jakes

"The remedy for life's broken pieces is not classes, workshops or books. Don't try to heal the broken pieces. Just forgive." – Iyanla Vanzant

Take time to answer these questions:

What guilt do you still carry?

How can you shift your perspective?

What can you do to be nice to yourself?

Ignore Your Feelings

Ignoring your feelings may sound completely crazy. It seems to be the *opposite* of what people tell us:

"Trust your gut."

"I can't help what I feel."

"Follow your heart."

I say ignore your feelings—this may be a piece of advice that no one's ever given you before. In most cases, acting on your feelings, reacting in a split second, will get you in trouble.

The guy you work with pissed you off. You felt like punching him, so you did… you followed your feelings. Yes, it may have felt good in the moment. Yes, he may have even deserved it. But giving into your feelings and punching him may lead you to a string of "bad luck."

You lose your job. You can't pay your car payment. You can't support your family. On top of it all, he's pressing charges, all because you followed your feelings.

Even now, you may be blaming him for this these things. But you had a choice in that moment, and you chose to act based on your feelings.

Our feelings lie to us. That immediate instinct to lash out is the darkness, your demon, the negative ego. It acts out of fear and anger.

Any reaction you have that is not from love is the wrong reaction. You must remember you cannot control how other people behave, you can only control how you respond.

The Light/God/Source wants you to turn the other cheek. The Light wants you to use empathy to forgive your aggressor and self-awareness to be the observer of your own responses.

Worried that people will judge you and think you are weak?

The only opinion that matters is your opinion. The only judgment you should be worried about is your own judgment.

Let's try another situation where you should ignore your feelings.

If you look in the mirror and feel you are fat and ugly, or you hate yourself and feel you are completely unlovable, look around. You have friends and family who think you are beautiful, wonderful and completely lovable.

Are they all crazy? Are they *all* wrong? How is it feasible all the loving people in your life are wrong and you are right?

Consider the possibility that *you* are wrong. Look at yourself—you *are* beautiful and lovable. God created you perfect. You are created in His image. He has made you exactly who you need to be to fulfill your purpose in this life. Your worth is immeasurable.

Now, be nice to yourself.

Ignore your feelings. Ignore the voice that screams at you, "He can't treat you like that. You need to get even with him."

Shut down the negative thoughts that say you are ugly or unlovable, or that hold you back from positive action.

Say to yourself, "I reject that reality. The darkness will not win this argument because I refuse to believe your lies. I am a child of the Light, and I am beautiful, lovable and peaceful."

The more you do this, the better you will get at it. It's like a muscle you build up by using it. The more you reject that stream of constant criticism, goading and lies, the easier it will be to do the right thing, think the right way, and be right with God.

Those dark, negative thoughts are the result of a lifetime of societal conditioning and trauma creating incorrect core beliefs that produce a negative inner narrative. Psychology calls it the negative ego; Christianity would call it the devil or demons. Some call it the dark night of the soul. My friend and artist Mary Josephine calls it "The Inner Asshole."

Whatever you want to call it, it looks for our weaknesses and exploits them. If you have a quick temper, it will push you to explode with rage.

If you lack confidence, it will nip away at your self-worth.

If you are jealous, it will find a way to twist all situations to look like you are being betrayed.

No matter what your personal situation is, the inner asshole can always find a way to use it and pull you deeper into the dark pit of anger and depression.

When you hear that voice, you must condition yourself to notice and realize it's not you. The voice, that negative narrative, creates a separate voice from your own. Your purpose in this life is to overcome that voice. Notice when it rears its ugly head and look at your behavior. Correct your incorrect core beliefs.

When the inner asshole speaks, it's usually because it has found a weakness in you. Examine that weakness. Recognize that weakness and fix it like plugging a hole in the dam. Use that darkness to your advantage and turn it around.

Pray, meditate, and center yourself.

Ask the Light for help. "I'm having an issue in this area. Please help me heal my pain and recognize when the inner asshole is speaking. Help me be self-aware and be the observer. I have faith that you are with me, and I am not alone."

2 Corinthians 10:5: "We demolish arguments and every pretension that sets itself up against the knowledge of God, and we take captive every thought to make it obedient to Christ."

"Hatred does not cease by hatred, but only by love; this is the eternal rule." – Buddha

"In a controversy, the instant we feel anger we have already ceased striving for the truth and have begun striving for ourselves". – Buddha

"You will not be punished for your anger, you will be punished by your anger." – Buddha

"Holding on to anger is like grasping a hot coal with the intent of throwing it at someone else; you are the one who gets burned." – Buddha

"It is better to conquer yourself than to win a thousand battles. Then the victory is yours. It cannot be taken from you, not by angels or by demons, heaven or hell." – Buddha

"All wrong-doing arises because of mind. If mind is transformed can wrong-doing remain?" – Buddha

Take time to answer these questions:

What emotions rise up uninvited when you are triggered?

Do you see a pattern?

Can you interrupt that pattern with counterthoughts?

Set Your Mind

What does that mean, really?

What am I talking about?

Basically, setting your mind is the equivalent to visualizing your future and creating your own reality. Books like *The Secret* tell us that by visualizing our future and really believing it, we can make it come true. They tell us if we really focus on it, through affirmations and vision boards and so forth, that we can make it happen.

When you look around at your reality, it's hard to imagine how to get from point A to point B, from your apartment to your mansion, from your minimum wage job to your riches, from your Kia to your Benz. Society and the self-help gurus make it sound so easy. Visualize what you want, believe it will happen, and *poof,* it happens. They don't tell you how to hold onto your vision after a week, a month, or a year.

How do you do it? How do you make the magic happen? How do you *poof*?

Our thoughts create frequencies, similar to a radio broadcaster. Our frequency is always creating reality around us. Our thoughts, our intentions, and our actions are all attracting and creating the world around us. The Law of Attraction has hundreds, maybe thousands, of articles, books, videos and classes on it. But really, it's just as simple as utilizing the Divine within you and shifting your frequency. Pay attention to your thoughts, actions and words. Focus on the change you want to see. Be the change. Set your mind.

You are connected to the Divine every moment of every day.

The Light knows your vision. The Light hears your plans. The Light gets you from here to there. The Light is how it happens.

Now, you can't just ask and then wait. Have you ever heard the saying, "God helps those who help themselves?"

This is literal. You cannot just wait for the Universe to make your dreams come true. Yes, visualize, manifest, meditate, or pray. Whatever works for you. But you must also prepare.

I heard preacher and motivational speaker Devon Franklin say on Oprah there are only two things we have control over—how we prepare and how we react; God/the Light/Source controls the rest. You must do the work on your end.

If you want a record contract, pray for it, but continue to only make music in your garage, then you're not doing your part! Get out there, get seen, make music and pray or meditate every day.

What you did yesterday got you here. What you do today gets you there.

Tell the Universe you will serve. Ask for the opportunity. Believe in yourself. Believe in the Divine. Believe it will happen.

Keep your mind set.

The Divine is the missing piece in the visualization puzzle. If you can believe that the Universe/Light/God will make it happen, then you can hold onto your vision for as long as it takes.

Now, it may not be on your schedule. The Universe has its own timetable and may need to prepare you to go through all the hard times associated with success and fame.

The hard times prepare you for the good times. Every hard time teaches you a lesson you will need when you vision comes true.

Televangelist Joel Osteen says, "Nothing happens *to* you; it happens *for* you."

Sometimes, the Universe has a different idea of what our purpose is. Set your mind and know you are not alone. The Light hears your voice and is already working to make your dreams come true!

John 15:7: "If you remain in me and my words remain in you, ask whatever you wish, and it will be done for you."

Numbers 14:28: "So tell them, 'As surely as I live, declares the Lord, I will do to you the very thing I heard you say."

Romans 12:2: "Do not conform to the pattern of this world but be transformed by the renewing of your mind. Then you will be able to test and approve what God's will is—his good, pleasing and perfect will."

Ephesians 4:22-24: "You were taught, with regard to your former way of life, to put off your old self, which is being corrupted by its deceitful desires.; to be made new in the attitude of your minds; and to put on the new self, created to be like God in true righteousness and holiness."

2 Corinthians 10:5: "We demolish arguments and every pretension that sets itself up against the knowledge of God, and we take captive every thought to make it obedient to Christ."

"We are shaped by our thoughts; we become what we think. When the mind is pure, joy follows like a shadow that never leaves." – Buddha

"The wise ones fashioned speech with their thought, sifting it as grain is sifted through a sieve." – Buddha

"He who walks in the eightfold noble path with unswerving determination is sure to reach Nirvana." – Buddha

"Sometimes I thank God for unanswered prayers." – Garth Brooks

Take time to answer these questions:

Do you see any patterns in your thinking that may be counterproductive?

How can you use self-awareness to affect your mindset?

Have Faith

This may be the most important part and the most difficult. It's the piece of the puzzle that makes all the other pieces fit. Without faith, the other puzzle pieces will not click into place.

What is faith?

I would compare faith to positive thinking. Always walking on the sunny side of the street, looking for the silver lining.

Faith is knowing and believing that you are not alone—even when you are at your loneliest.

Faith is being nice to people who don't deserve it, including yourself.

Faith is forgiving yourself, forgiving others and letting go of the past—even if you were terribly wrong or have been terribly wronged.

Faith is ignoring your feelings, especially when they are telling you you'll never amount to anything.

Faith is keeping your mind set, no matter what obstacles are in your way.

The crucial thing about faith is the more you have, the happier your ending, the easier your joy will come, and the bigger your reward. There is a direct correlation between the strength of your faith and a happy ending. No matter what, you must behave as if the future you want is a sure thing, designed for your benefit and orchestrated by you and the Universe.

Faith is what manifests the reality of your vision. By plugging your Divine connection into the equation, you amp up the manifestation of your visions. Having faith in the Light is what will help you utilize all of the steps to come to a space of unconditional love of Self and others and to embrace the great "I Am" within you.

James 1:6: "But when you ask, you must believe and not doubt, because the one who doubts is like a wave of the sea, blown and tossed by the wind."

Hebrews 10:35-36: "So do not throw away your confidence; it will be richly rewarded. You need to persevere so that when you have done the will of God, you will receive what he has promised."

Hebrews 11:1: "Now faith is confidence in what we hope for and assurance about what we do not see."

Isaiah 61:7: "Instead of your shame you will receive a double portion, and instead of disgrace you will rejoice in your inheritance. And so you will inherit a double portion in your land, and everlasting joy will be yours."

Matthew 21:22: "If you believe, you will receive whatever you ask for in prayer."

Mark 11:24: "Therefore I tell you, whatever you ask for in prayer, believe that you have received it, and it will be yours."

Ezekiel 11:19: "I will give them an undivided heart and put a new spirit in them; I will remove from them their heart of stone and give them a heart of flesh."

Hebrews 12:11: "No discipline seems pleasant at the time, but painful. Later on, however, it produces a harvest of righteousness and peace for those who have been trained by it."

John 15:7: "If you remain in me and my words remain in you, ask whatever you wish, and it will be done for you."

Psalm 136: "Give thanks to the Lord, for he is good. His love endures forever."

Take time to answer this question:

How can you expand your faith in everyday life?

Hang in There

I'm not going to sugarcoat it. This process is not always going to be easy. There may be parts that come naturally. There may be parts that you struggle with but hang in there.

You can conquer the darkness within you, the shadow self, and the primal place of pain.

You can persevere the 'Dark Night of the Soul.'

You can find peace.

You can release the past.

You can forgive those who have hurt you.

When you feel weak or slip into old habits, reread the step that applies to your situation. Read the scriptures and quotes for help. Give yourself a hug and love yourself in the hard times.

Know the Light/God/Divine is always with you. Have faith the Divine will open your heart and help you live through unconditional love, empathy and compassion.

I know you can do this.

I have faith in you, and I have faith in the Divine Light that we share!

I work on myself every day through my own self-awareness, paying attention to my emotions and thought pattern. Every moment of every day I make a choice. If I choose wisely, I move closer to my path and purpose. If I make a wrong choice, I take a breath. I ask for forgiveness. I realize maybe my wrong choice was necessary. I learn what I am supposed to learn from it. I move on without shame, blame or self judgement.

<u>1 John 4:7-8</u>: "Beloved, let us love one another, for love is from God, and whoever loves has been born of God and knows God. Anyone who does not love does not know God, because God is love."

<u>1 John 3:1</u>: "See what kind of love the Father has given to us, that we should be called children of God; and so we are. The reason why the world does not know us is that it did not know him."

Jeremiah 29:11: "For I know the plans I have for you, declares the LORD, plans for welfare and not for evil, to give you a future and a hope."

This is the most important part of making a direct connection with the Divine within you and Unleashing Your Light.

Love

Love, love, love, love, love!

We must show love to each other, and we must show love to ourselves. The power of love (no I'm not quoting Huey Lewis) is the most powerful emotion in the universe. It's a transformative, life changing power.

Every one of the stops along the road map I've outlined is a way for you to make the switch to act out of love and only love. Every stop is another way to tell you to be loving to each other. Be loving to yourself. To find peace, to find joy, to find God/Light Divine, to find the light, you *must* find love. You must act in love. You must react from love. You must live in love each moment of each day.

Love is the secret.

Love is the cure.

Love is the answer.

<u>John 13:34-35</u>: "A new commandment I give to you, that you love one another: just as I have loved you, you also are to love one another. By this all people will know that you are my disciples, if you have love for one another."

You can find peace.

You can be happy.

You are not alone.

The Light is always with you.

Be kind and compassionate.

Heal with forgiveness and empathy.

Love yourself unconditionally. Embrace the "I Am" within you.

Unleash Your Light.

About the Author

li Cara is a Spiritual Speaker, Intuitive Empath, and Channeler, blessed in her Awakening with a simple message from Divine: simple things we can do every day to access the Divine within. li relays this message in a simple, compassionate way, using her own experiences and transformation as a part of the journey. She currently broadcasts her show, Unleash Your Light, weekly on Facebook live, sharing insight into using and embodying empathy, compassion and unconditional love toward others and toward ourselves to transform our everyday lives.

In her spare time, li loves creating art and crystal jewelry, singing and writing songs, reading, visiting the mountains, hanging out with her kids, watching terrible movies and cuddling with her cats.

Watch Unleash Your Light LIVE on Facebook at Facebook.com/unleashyourlight

Thursdays at 10am EST

Li Cara is available for speaking, podcasts, video interviews and more.

Visit UnleashYourLight.org for more information or email li at hello@UnleashYourLight.org.

See excerpt from Simple Spirituality of Self

Spirituality gets a bad rap.

Too often when people hear the word spirituality, they think hippies, love and light, crystals, New Age and rituals.

They're thinking of people burning candles and spinning in circles, chanting under a full moon.

Now, do some people who practice spirituality do all that? Yes.

Do *all* people who practice spirituality do that? No.

Some people who practice spirituality are Christian. Some people who practice spirituality are Jewish. Some people who practice spirituality are Buddhist. Some people who practice spirituality are Muslim. Some people who practice spirituality don't prescribe to any particular religion. In fact, some people who practice spirituality think all religions are BS.

Spirituality, in and of itself, is merely the belief that we are more than flesh and blood, that we are more than just these bodies. We are more than the lives that we lead. Spirituality merely says we are the spirit within the body. We are the soul who lives inside the mortal vessel that is our body. Spirituality is the belief that the soul is something bigger than the short mortal life we live. It is the belief the soul is connected to something bigger; a puzzle to which we don't have all the pieces.

Spirituality simply says I accept I am a small piece of something bigger.

I accept I am connected to a whole.

I am a piece of the light.

I am a piece of God.

Spirituality simply says I am connected to all living things, and all living things are connected to me.

Spirituality says there's more to this world than what we see with our eyes, what we feel with our hands and what we hear with our ears.

Spirituality is the acceptance of our place in this world, as a piece of this world; a living breathing extension of the energy that makes up every corner of this beautiful world.

How can you use spirituality to help you in your everyday life?

Because that's kind of the point, right?

We live an everyday life.

Every day we get up. Every day we get our kids ready for school, or we get ourselves ready for work. Every day we get in our cars, or we get on public transportation. Every day we get in the rat race. We get on the hamster wheel. We get on the grind. Every day we have to go into the world and do our job. We do what we're supposed to do and live the life society says we are supposed to live.

How can we use spirituality to make our lives **more** than just this mundane life? Too many of us walk around feeling empty, feeling lost; knowing there's more to life than this grind; knowing there's more than this hamster wheel. So many of us know there is more; but don't know what that **more** is. So many of us don't know how to access that **more.**

www.ingramcontent.com/pod-product-compliance
Lightning Source LLC
Chambersburg PA
CBHW052102110526
44591CB00013B/2316